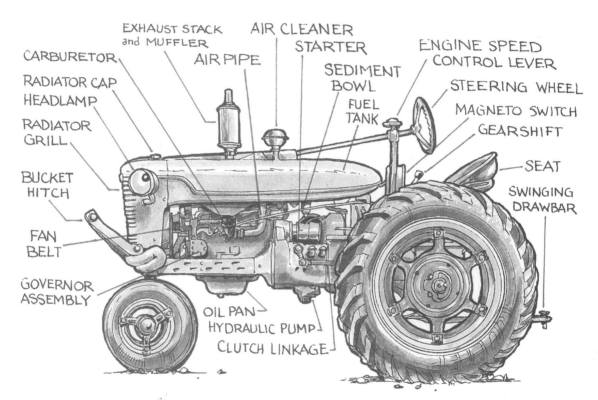

Tractor Mac

Tractor Mac
SAVES CHRISTMAS
written and illustrated by Billy Steers

Billy Steers
2009

Snow fell in big fat flakes and blanketed Stony Meadow Farm. Tractor Mac knew the snow was coming before it started. He had seen the halo around the moon the night before and Farmer Bill had attached the wheel weights, tire chains, and bucket loader for moving snow.

Mac could see many different types of tracks in the fast falling snow. He could see small bird tracks and the larger tracks of Carla the chicken and the other hens.

"I bet the snowman has turned them into snow sculptures," said Walter the goat. "Haven't you heard that snowmen come to life during blizzards?"

"Oh foo, Walter", grunted Margot the cow. "Every time there is a rumble of thunder or a hint of snow you think something bad is lurking out there."

"There IS something lurking out there!" cried Walter, "and it's coming closer!" Everyone strained to see through the blinding snow.

"A SNOWMAN'S COME TO LIFE!" shrieked Margot. "RUN FOR THE BARN!!"

Snow flew in all directions as animals exploded through the drifts and ran for shelter. The shadowy, snowy figure approached Tractor Mac.

"H'lo Mac." Farmer Bill said. Tractor Mac smiled with relief. "Poor Sibley's tuckered out and stuck in the snow" Farmer Bill said. "I've grabbed some blankets and supplies. If we hurry, we can rescue Sibley and save the tree lighting."

"We're heading to the coop," clucked Carla.
"It's getting too deep!" Mac used his big treads
to make a tire track path for his friends.

Mac saw the tracks of the sheep in the snow. "It's going to get much deeper" a voice said. It was Sam the Ram. "They may have to cancel the town tree lighting tonight," he said shaking the snow from his horns.

Swoosh! Whoosh! went the blowing snow. It was slow moving in the thick drifts. Snow packed tight around Tractor Mac's wheels and he could barely feel the road beneath his tires.

They reached the Christmas tree on the sled. "I'm glad you're here, Mac," said Sibley. "I'm tired and I can't pull this tree further by myself."

Mac went straight to work.
   Scoop – Push – Dump!
   Scoop – Push – Dump!
He soon had Sibley out of the snow bank.

The two friends tugged the heavy load towards town till they came
upon one of the town dump trucks stuck in a snow drift.
"We were trying to clear the roads to the Christmas
tree lighting," said the driver.

    Scoop – Push – Dump!

Mac had them unstuck soon.

Further along they came upon the town fire truck stuck fast in a gulley. "We have the lights and the decorations for the tree," said the volunteer firemen.

    Scoop – Push – Dump!

Mac dug the fire truck out. "Thanks, Mac!" said Number Three the fire truck. "I felt a little silly being a rescuer needing rescuing!"

Closer to town they found a school bus unable to move. "We were bringing families to the tree lighting," said the bus driver. Farmer Bill shared his blankets with the passengers and…

Scoop – Push – Dump!

Tractor Mac freed the bus from the snow.

As Sibley and Mac pulled the big tree to the center of the town green, people gathered around with shovels, brooms, and warm food. Paper bags with lit candles inside helped guide the way.

Everyone cheered as the beautiful evergreen was hoisted up, lit, and decorated. People sang carols and there was hot cider, hot cocoa and cookies and cakes for everyone.

"How could they cancel the tree lighting?" Mac asked. "What would Christmas be without the town tree lighting?" Mac remembered all the carols sung and the hot cocoa and gingerbread treats for the children that were part of the town tree lighting.

"The snow is falling too
fast! If they can't clear
the roads, the people can't
make it to the town center
for the celebration," said Sam.
Mac could see the snow was up
to the bottom rung on the fence.
"Moo!" called Margot
the cow. "I'm worried about
Sibley! Farmer Bill harnessed
him up hours ago to go and get the
town Christmas tree from the tree lot. I
haven't seen them go by the farm towards
town yet."

The lights reflected off the slowing snowstorm and calm filled the night. Sibley declared, "I think we will always remember this year as the one when Tractor Mac saved Christmas!"

Billy Steers is an author, illustrator, and pilot. In addition to the Tractor Mac series, he has worked on forty other children's books. Mr. Steers had horses and sheep on the farm where he grew up in Roxbury, Connecticut. Married with three sons, he still lives in Roxbury.

![Tractor Mac]()
Tractor Mac™

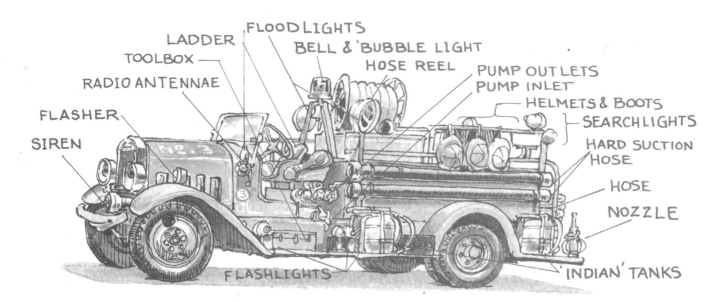

FLOOD LIGHTS
LADDER
BELL & BUBBLE LIGHT
TOOLBOX
HOSE REEL
RADIO ANTENNAE
PUMP OUTLETS
PUMP INLET
FLASHER
HELMETS & BOOTS
SIREN
SEARCH LIGHTS
HARD SUCTION HOSE
HOSE
NOZZLE
FLASHLIGHTS
'INDIAN' TANKS

Number Three